Goodies for Guitar

Frances Turnbull

Published by Musicaliti® Publishers
575 Tonge Moor Road, Bolton, BL2 3BN

Copyright © 2016 Musicaliti
ISBN 978-1-907935-72-5

All rights reserved. No part of this publication may be reproduced, stored in a retrieval system, or transmitted by any means, mechanical, photocopying, recording or otherwise, without the prior permission of the copyright holder.

Index of Songs

Around the Buttercup	15
Bought me a Cat	23
Bow Wow Wow	13
Built my Lady	26
Do Pity My Cases	27
Down the Road	28
Frosty Weather	12
G-Scale	30
Here Comes a Bluebird	20
How Many Miles	24
Hush Little Baby	9
Johnny Works	21
John Kinaker	16
No one in the House	23
Oats and Beans	10
Once a Man Fell	11
Pumpkin Pumpkin	25
Sally go round the Sun	14
This Way Valerie	29
Tideo Tideo	17
Who Did All the Baking?	18
Who's That?	22

Guitar Basics

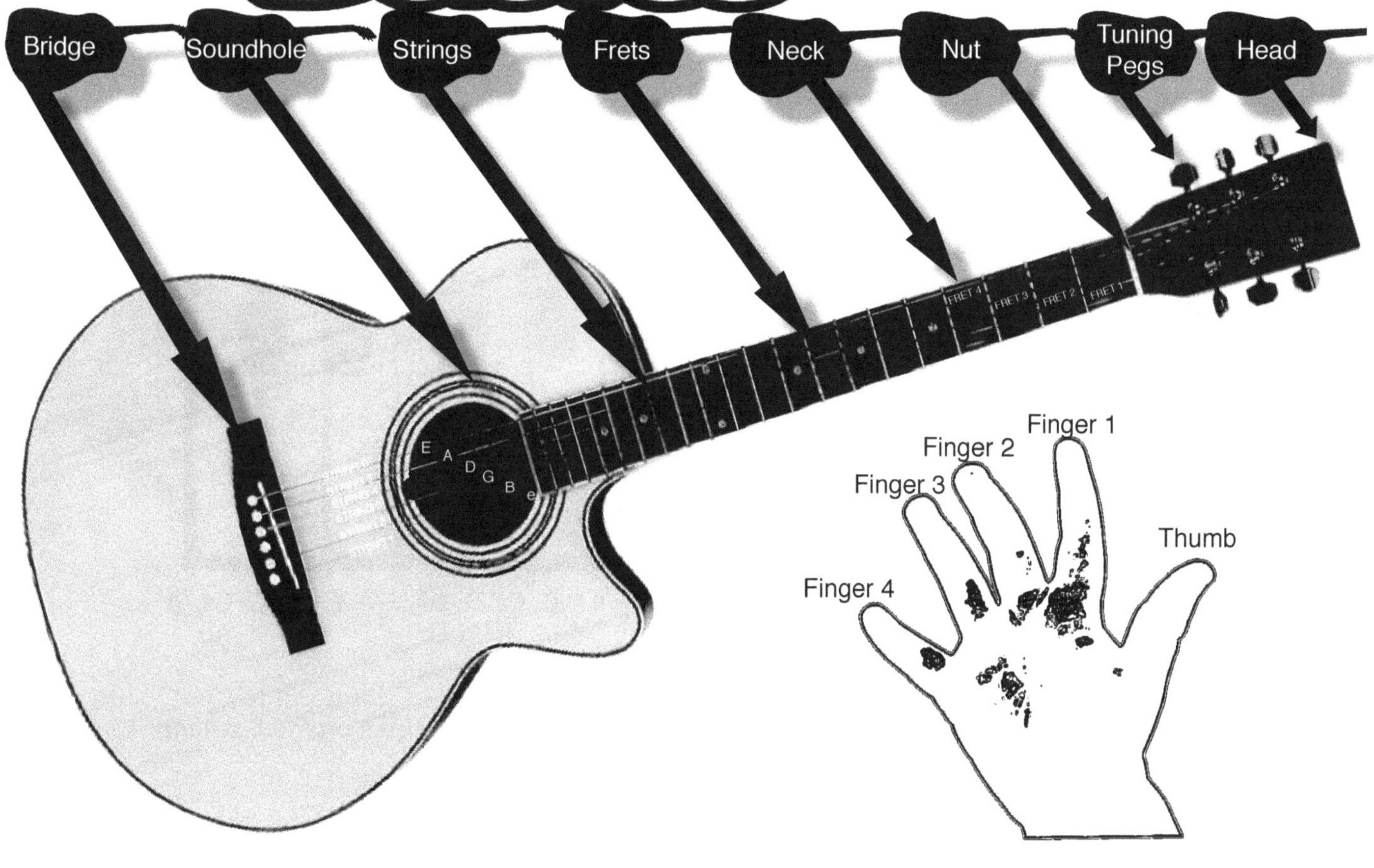

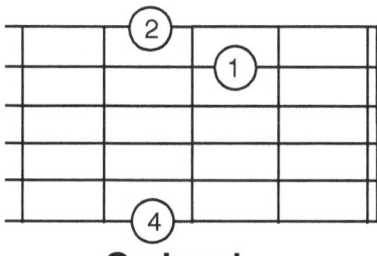
G chord

Guitar can be used to play tunes or **melodies** (one or a few notes at a time) or to accompany songs being sung - by playing all the strings with your fingers in the shape of a chord. The songs in this book are all in the chord of G. This means that you can play the G chord and sing along to the songs, or play the tune - it is a great skill to be able to do both! You could even have a guitar friend play the chord while you play the melody (tune) or the other way around! These pictures show the chords that we have used in this book. The numbers in circles show which finger to use!

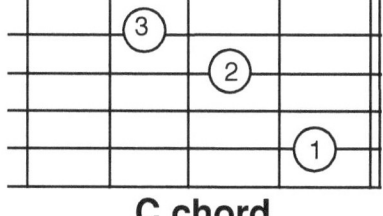
C chord

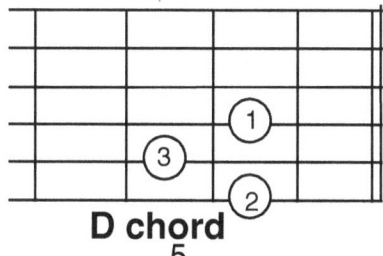
D chord

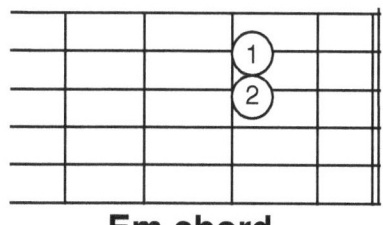
Em chord

How the notes work

The songs in this book are written in the **G scale**. Songs in the **green book** have the fewest notes as you get used to playing the notes of songs on the guitar, with more notes in **pink book**, **yellow book**, **blue book** and **orange book**.

The notes in a G scale are: **G, A, B, C, D, E, F#**. On a **piano**, they look like this:

Music notes: A A# B C C# D D# E F F# G G# A A# B   C C# D D# E   F F# G G# A
             Bb   Db   Eb   Gb   Ab   Bb   Db   Eb   Gb   Ab

On a **guitar**, they look like this:
(guitar strings start with different notes/letters, and this picture shows the notes on the E string)

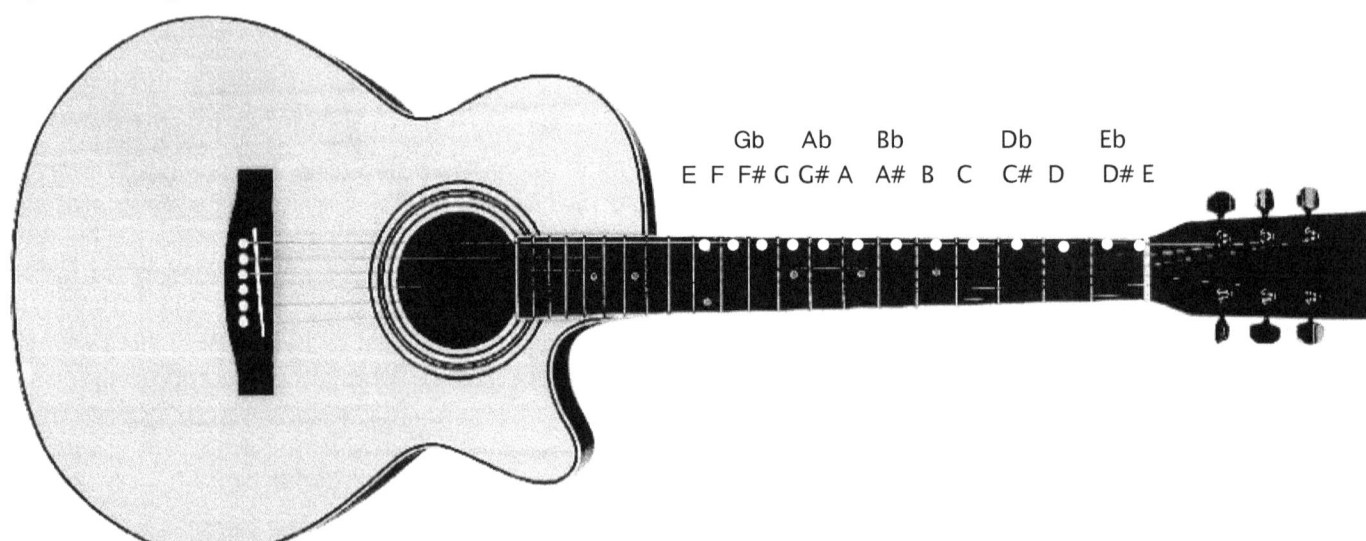

                                    Gb   Ab   Bb   Db   Eb
                                 E F F# G G# A A# B C   C# D   D# E

Scales have set gaps in between the notes, and the gaps between these notes determine when the black notes, or sharps and flats (also called accidentals) are used. Accidentals can be sharp (#) or flat (b), depending on the scale.

It's easy to focus on only playing the right notes, but we need to get the **long and short** beats right, too. It can be tricky to work out until we know what the lines and holes in the notes mean, so we can use **movement words** to remember how the beats sound. That way, you could say the movement words instead of the song words to remember how long to play the note!

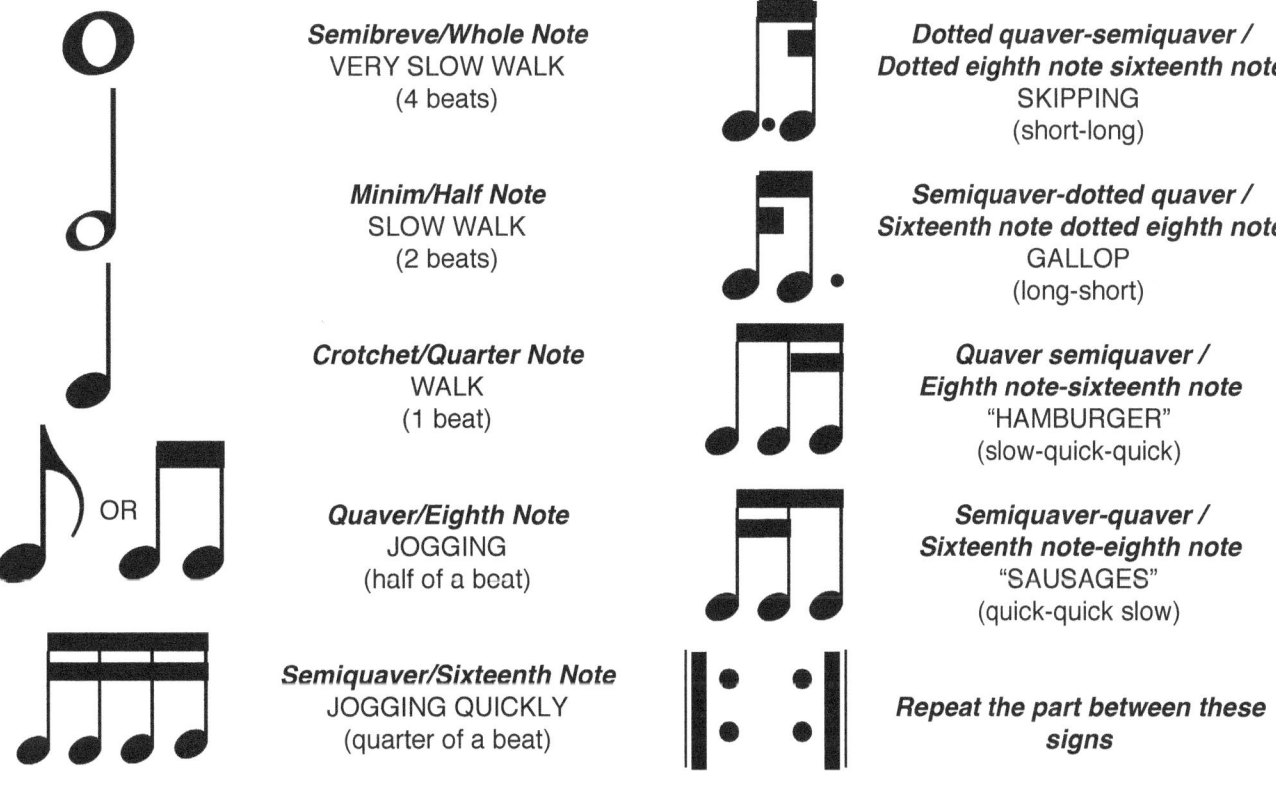

For example, if we sang the movement rhythms to "This Old Man", we would have:

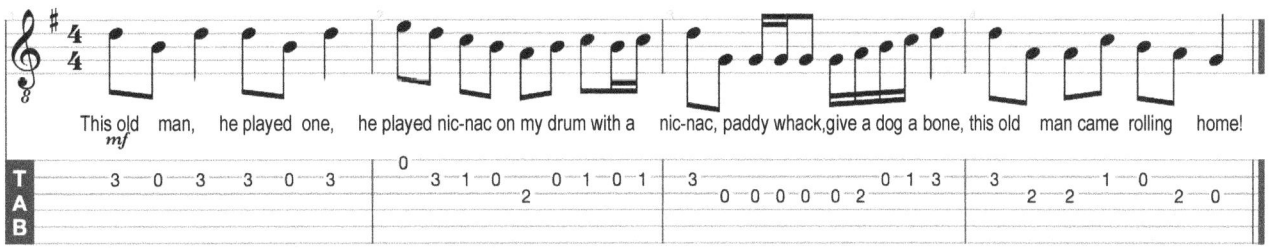

Give it a try before singing the songs!

These pages introduce songs with 5 notes, and the different lengths of beats used:

E is on the 1st open string
D is on the 2nd string, 3rd fret
B is on the 2nd open string
A is on the 3rd string, 2nd fret
G is on the 3rd open string
F# is on the 4th string, 4th fret
E is on the 4th string, 2nd fret

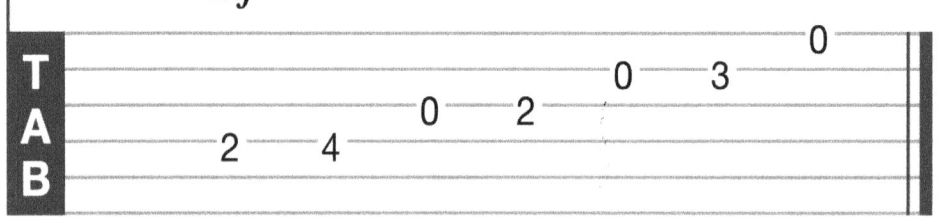

1st string
2nd string
3rd string
4th string
5th string
6th string

Semibreve/Whole Note
VERY SLOW WALK
(4 beats)

Minim/Half Note
SLOW WALK
(2 beats)

Crotchet/Quarter Note
WALK
(1 beat)

Quaver/Eighth Note
JOGGING
(half of a beat)

Semiquaver/Sixteenth Note
JOGGING QUICKLY
(quarter of a beat)

Dotted quaver-semiquaver / Dotted eighth note sixteenth note
SKIPPING
(short-long)

Semiquaver-dotted quaver / Sixteenth note dotted eighth note
GALLOP
(long-short)

Quaver semiquaver / Eighth note-sixteenth note
"HAMBURGER"
(slow-quick-quick)

Semiquaver-quaver / Sixteenth note-eighth note
"SAUSAGES"
(quick-quick slow)

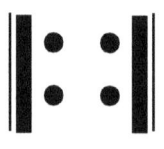

Repeat the part between these signs

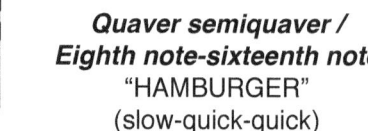

8

Hush Little Baby

Traditional

Guitar Standard Tuning
E-A-D-G-B-E

♩ = 120

Hush lit-tle ba-by, don't say a word, mamma's gon-na buy you a mo-king bird,

Next verse:

And if that mocking bird don't sing
Mamma's gonna buy you a diamond ring
If that diamond ring turns brass
Mamma's gonna buy you a looking glass
And if that looking glass gets broke
Mamma's gonna buy you a billy goat
If that billy goat don't pull
Mamma's gonna buy you a cart and bull
If that cart and bull turn over
Mamma's gonna buy you a dog named Rover
If that dog named Rover don't bark
Mamma's gonna buy you a horse and cart
And if that horse and cart fall down
You'll still be the sweetest little baby in town!

Guitar Standard Tuning
E-A-D-G-B-E
♩ = 120

Traditional

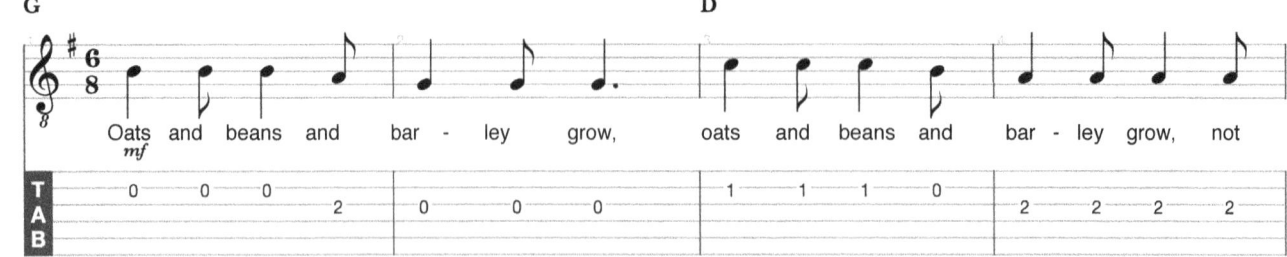

Oats and beans and bar - ley grow, oats and beans and bar - ley grow, not

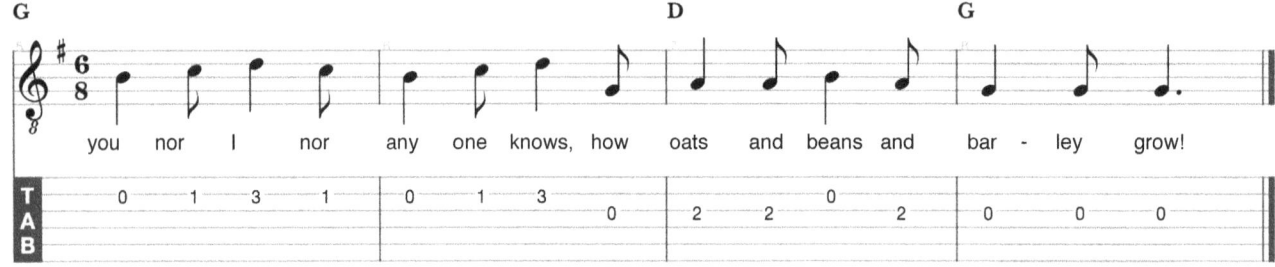

you nor I nor any one knows, how oats and beans and bar - ley grow!

Next verses:

First the farmer sows the seed
Stands up tall and takes his ease
Stamps his foot and claps his hands
And turns around to view the land

Waiting for a partner
Waiting for a partner
Not you nor I nor anyone knows I'm
Waiting for a partner

Dancing with a partner
Dancing with a partner
Both you and I and everyone knows I'm
Dancing with a partner

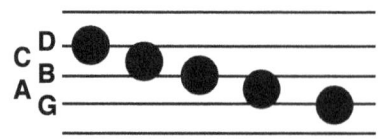

Guitar Standard Tuning
E-A-D-G-B-E
♩ = 120

Traditional

G

Once a man fell in a well, splish, splash, splosh it sounded, if he had not put it in, he would not have drown - ded!

mf

11

Frosty Weather

Guitar Standard Tuning
E-A-D-G-B-E
♩= 120

Traditional

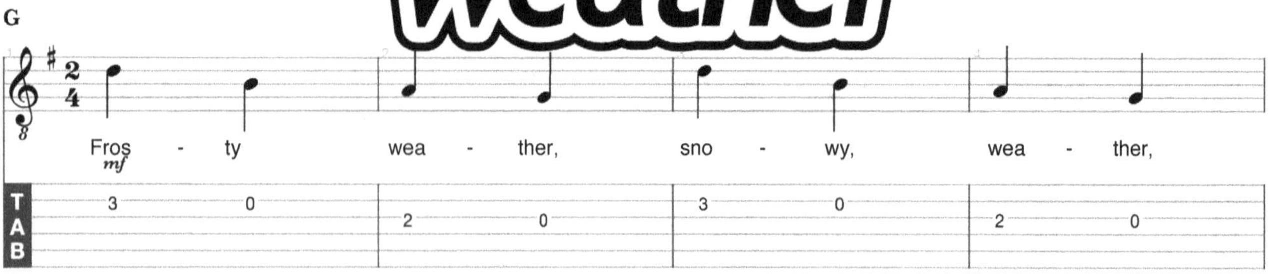

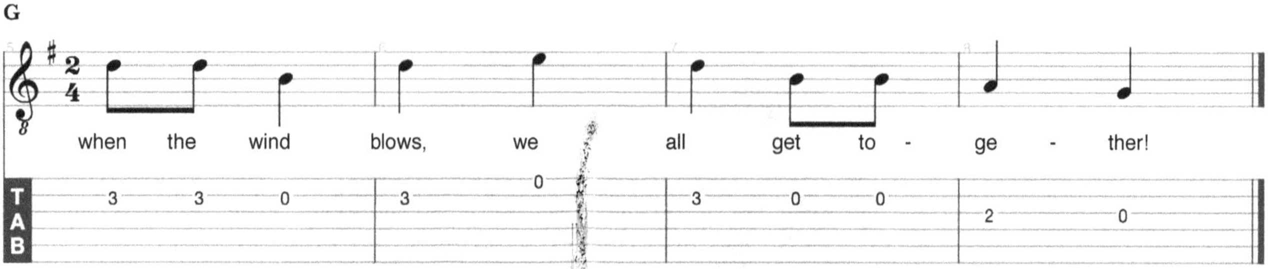

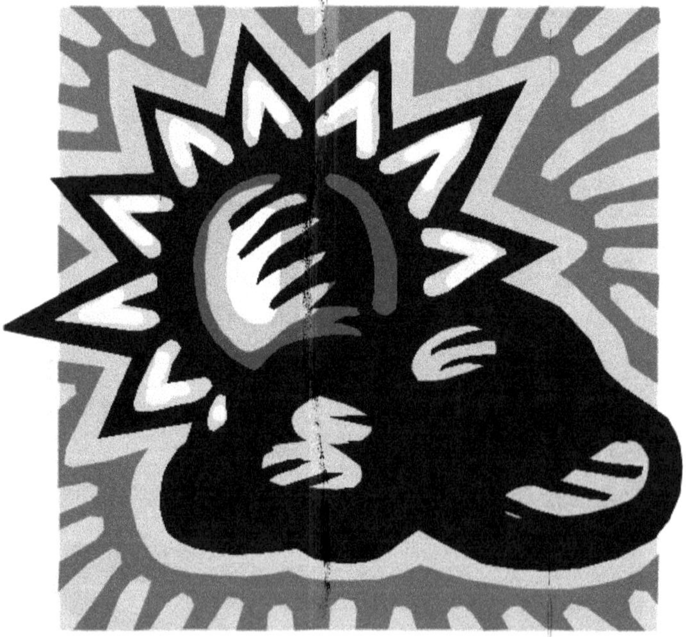

G
Fros - ty wea - ther, sno - wy, wea - ther,
mf
T
A
B
3 0 2 0 3 0 2 0

G
when the wind blows, we all get to - ge - ther!
T
A
B
3 3 0 3 0 3 0 0 2 0

Watch Out!

E
D
B
A
G

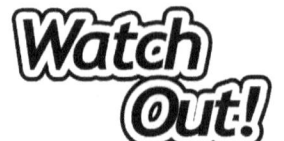

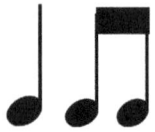

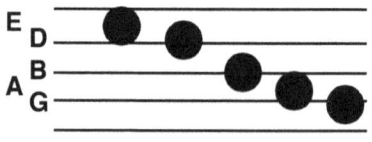

Guitar Standard Tuning
E-A-D-G-B-E
♩ = 120

Traditional

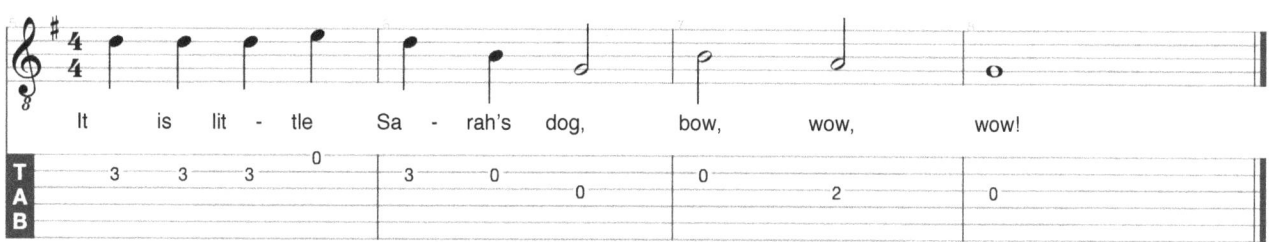

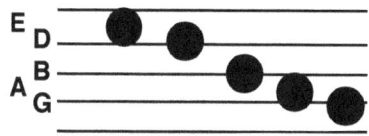

Guitar Standard Tuning
E-A-D-G-B-E
♩ = 120

Traditional

Guitar Standard Tuning
E-A-D-G-B-E
♩ = 120

Traditional

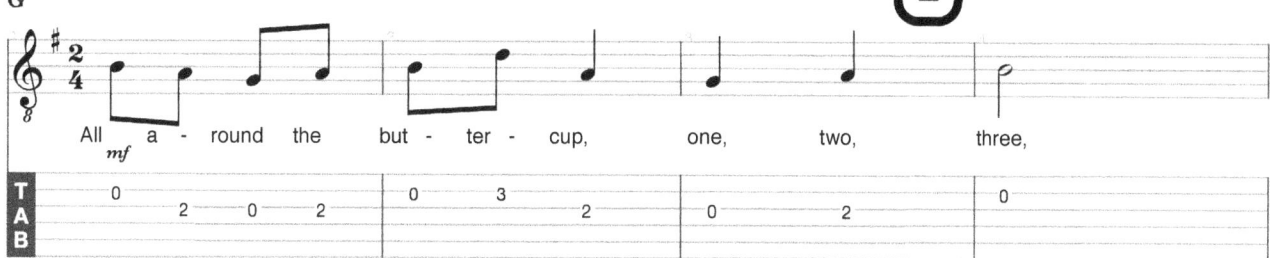

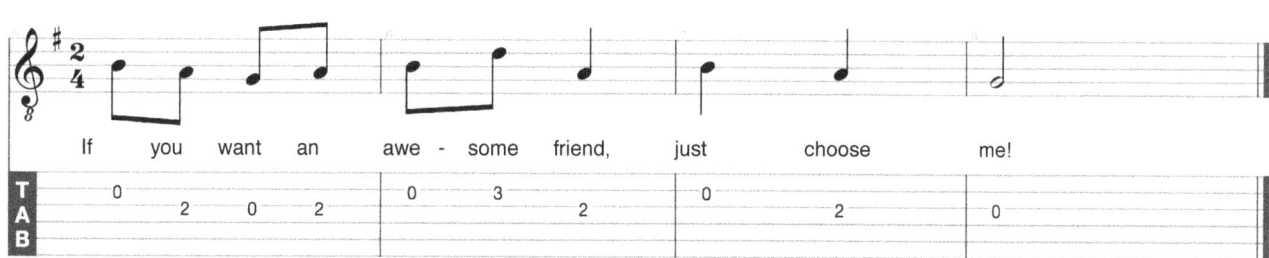

Guitar Standard Tuning
E-A-D-G-B-E
♩ = 120

Traditional

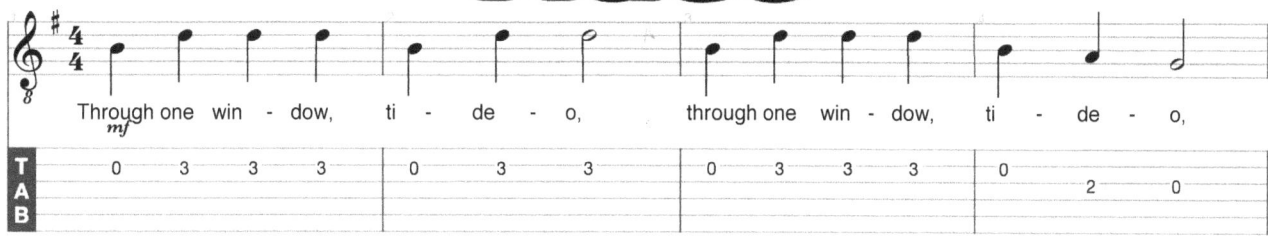

Through one win-dow, ti - de - o, through one win-dow, ti - de - o,

Through three win - dows, ti - de - o, jin - gle through the win - dow, ti - de - o,

Guitar Standard Tuning
E-A-D-G-B-E
♩ = 120

Traditional

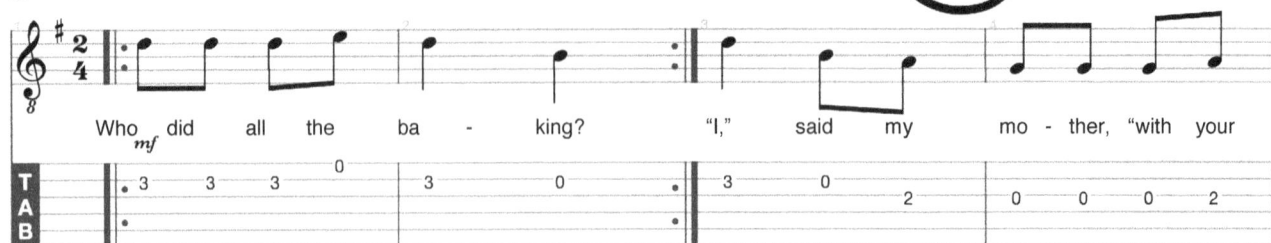

Who did all the ba - king? "I," said my mo - ther, "with your

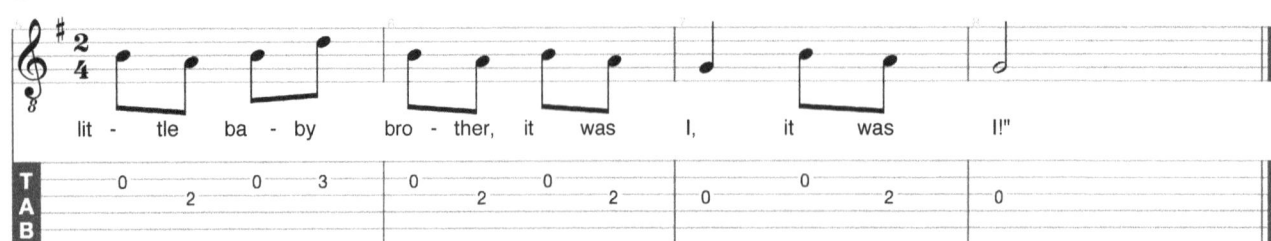

lit - tle ba - by bro - ther, it was I, it was I!"

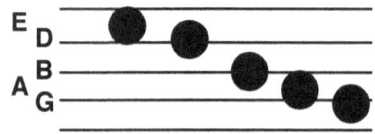

Here Comes a Bluebird

Guitar Standard Tuning
E-A-D-G-B-E
♩ = 120

Traditional

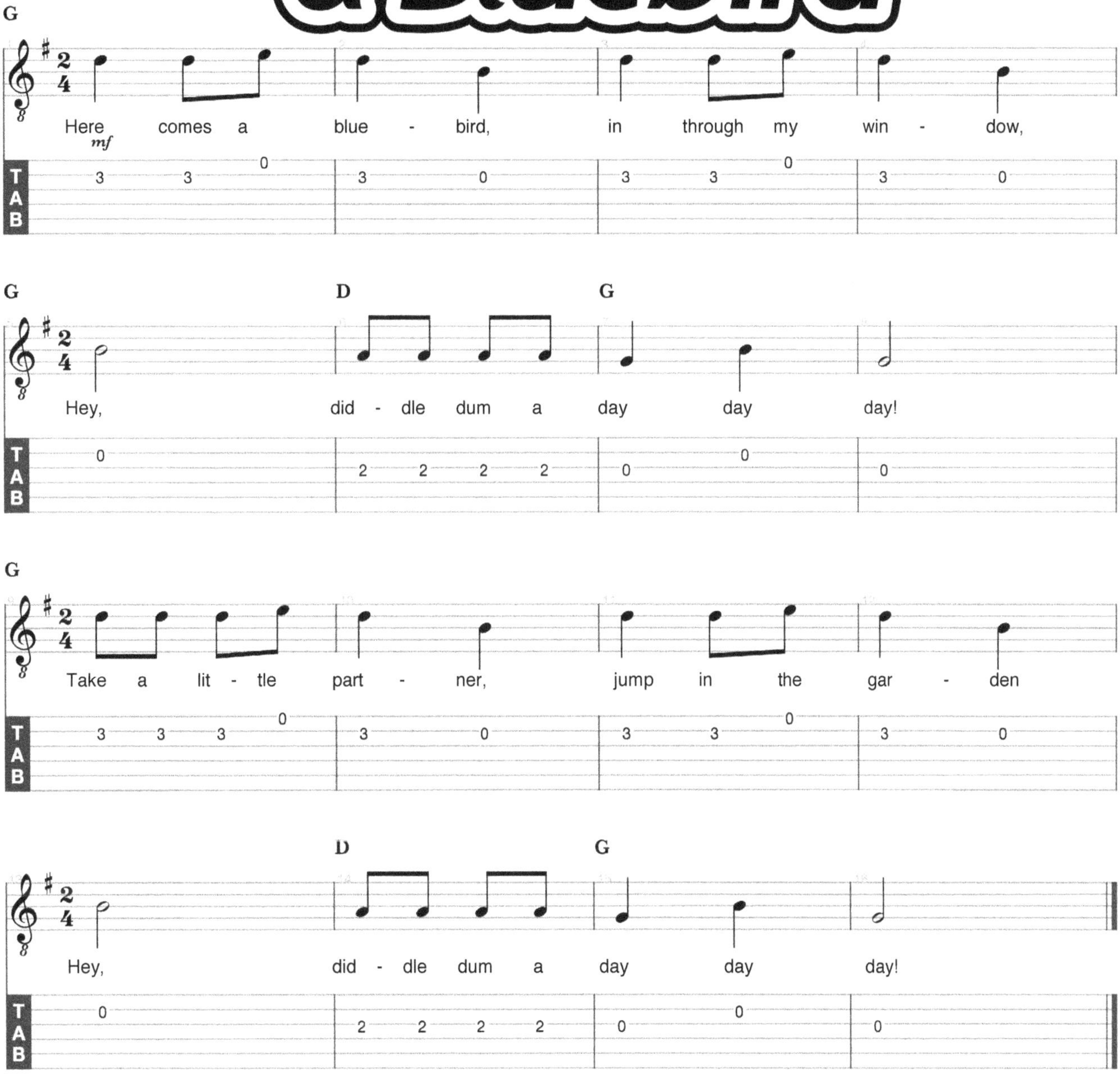
G
Here comes a blue - bird, in through my win - dow,
mf
G D G
Hey, did - dle dum a day day day!
G
Take a lit - tle part - ner, jump in the gar - den
D G
Hey, did - dle dum a day day day!

Watch Out!

E
D
B
A
G

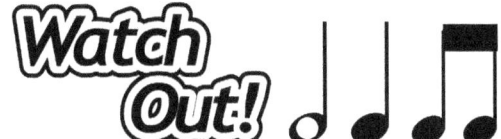

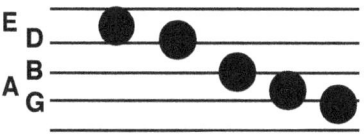

Johnny Works

Guitar Standard Tuning
E-A-D-G-B-E
♩ = 120

Traditional

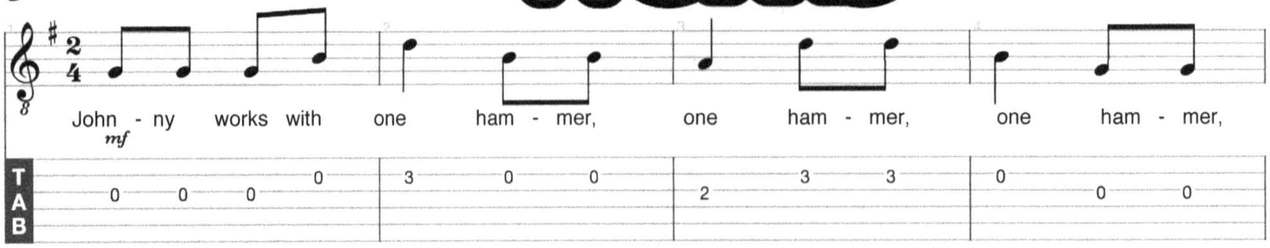

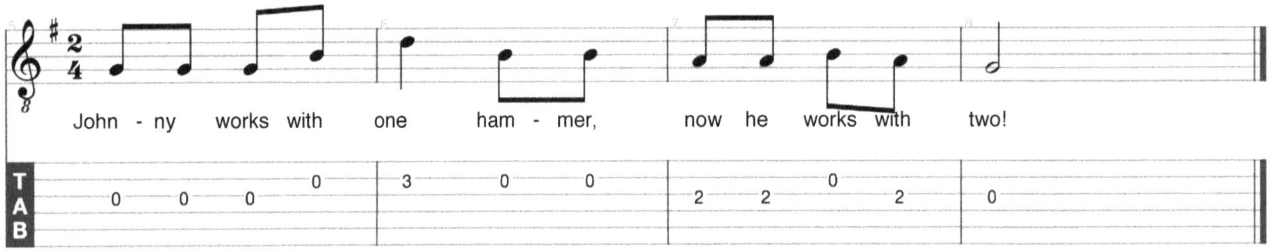

[Sheet music and tab notation]

Johnny works with one hammer, one hammer, one hammer,
Johnny works with one hammer, now he works with two!

Next verses:

Johnny works with two hammers
Two hammers, two hammers
Johnny works with two hammers
Now he works with three

Johnny works with three hammers
Two hammers, three hammers
Johnny works with three hammers
Now he works with four

Johnny works with four hammers
Two hammers, four hammers
Johnny works with four hammers
Now his work is done

Guitar Standard Tuning
E-A-D-G-B-E
♩ = 120

Traditional

G

Who's that knocking on my win-dow? who's that knocking on my door?

G

A - lly's knocking on my win-dow, A - lly's knocking on my door!

  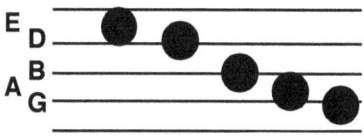

21

Bought me a Cat

Guitar Standard Tuning
E-A-D-G-B-E

♩ = 120

Traditional

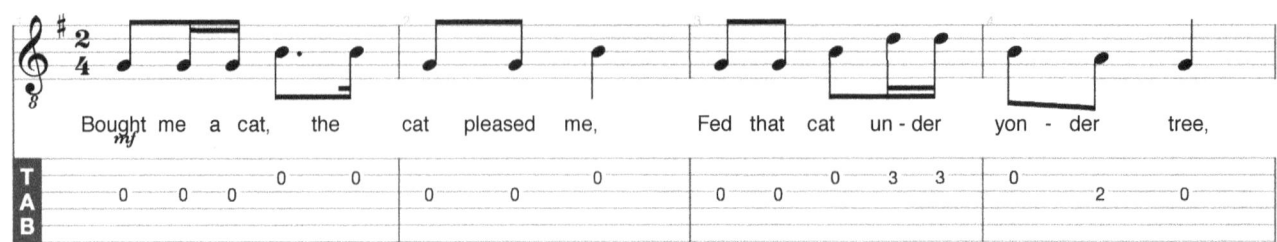

Bought me a cat, the cat pleased me, Fed that cat un-der yon-der tree,

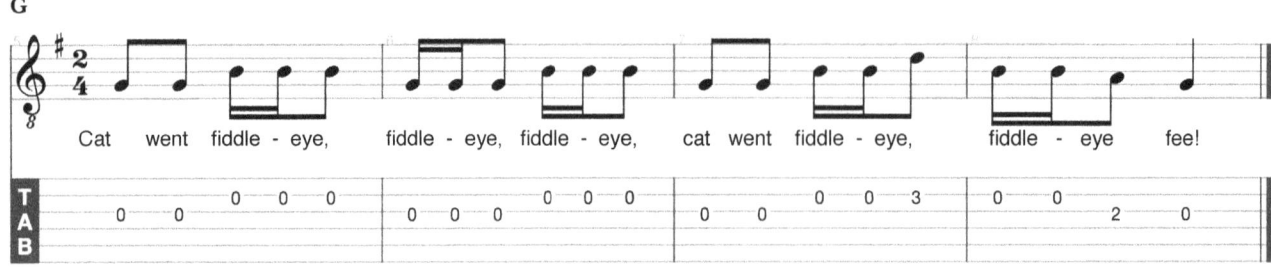

Cat went fiddle - eye, fiddle - eye, fiddle - eye, cat went fiddle - eye, fiddle - eye fee!

Next verses:

Bought me a hen, the hen pleased me
Fed my hen under yonder tree
Hen went chimmy-chuck, chimmy chuck
Cat went fiddle-eye, fiddle-eye fee

Bought me a duck, the duck pleased me
Fed that duck under yonder tree
Duck went quack quack
Hen went chimmy-chuck, chimmy chuck
Cat went fiddle-eye, fiddle-eye fee

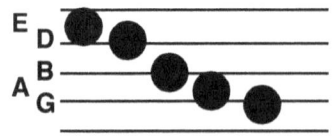

Guitar Standard Tuning
E-A-D-G-B-E
♩ = 120

Traditional

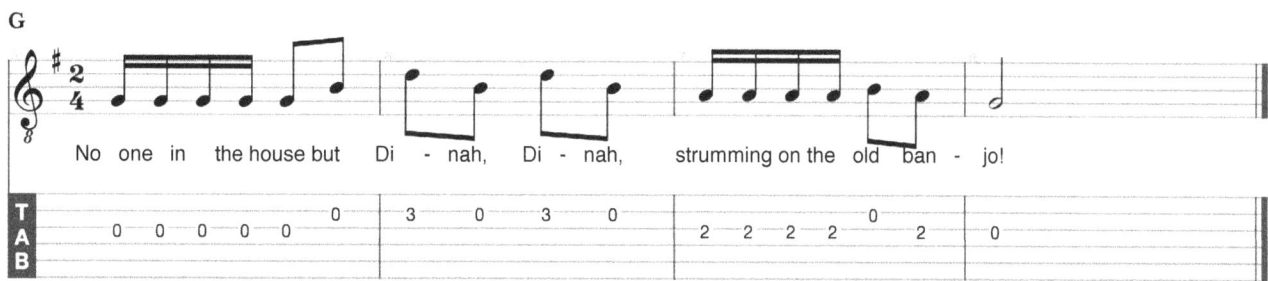

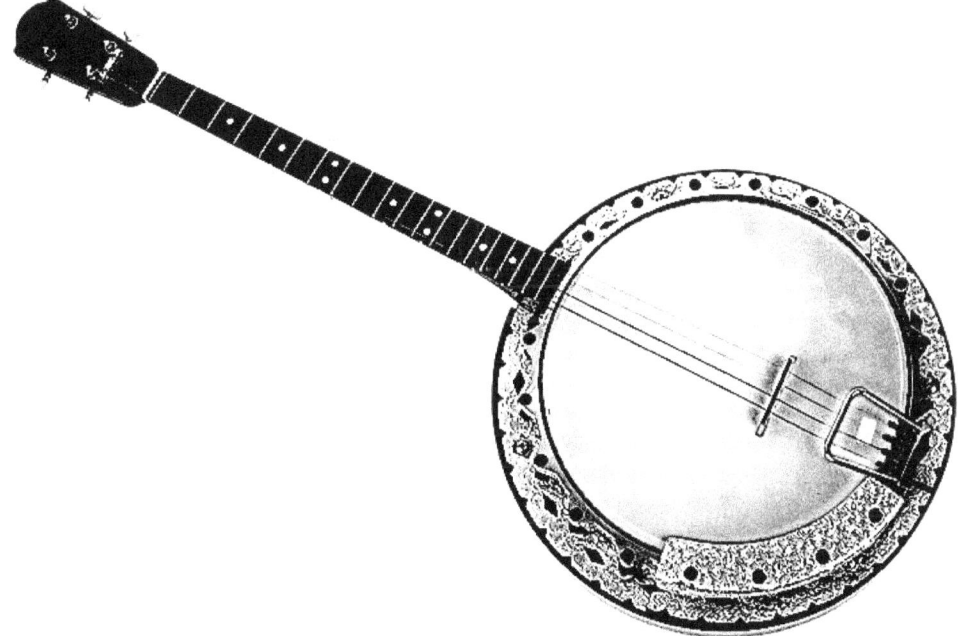

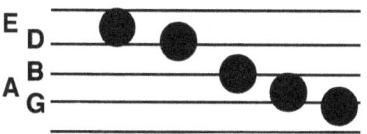

How Many Miles

Guitar Standard Tuning
E-A-D-G-B-E
♩= 120

Traditional

G
D
How many miles to Ba - by - lon? Three score and ten! Will
mf
G
I get there be - fore you do? Yes and back a - gain!
G
O - pen the gates and let us through! Not with - out a beck and bow!
Em
G
Here's the beck, here's the bow, o - pen the gates and let us through!
TAB

Watch Out!

E
D
B
A
G

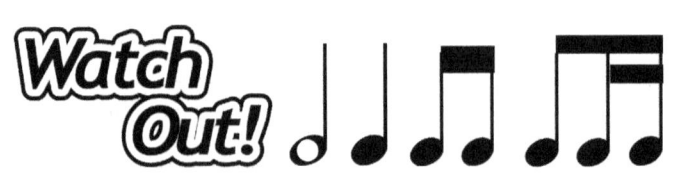

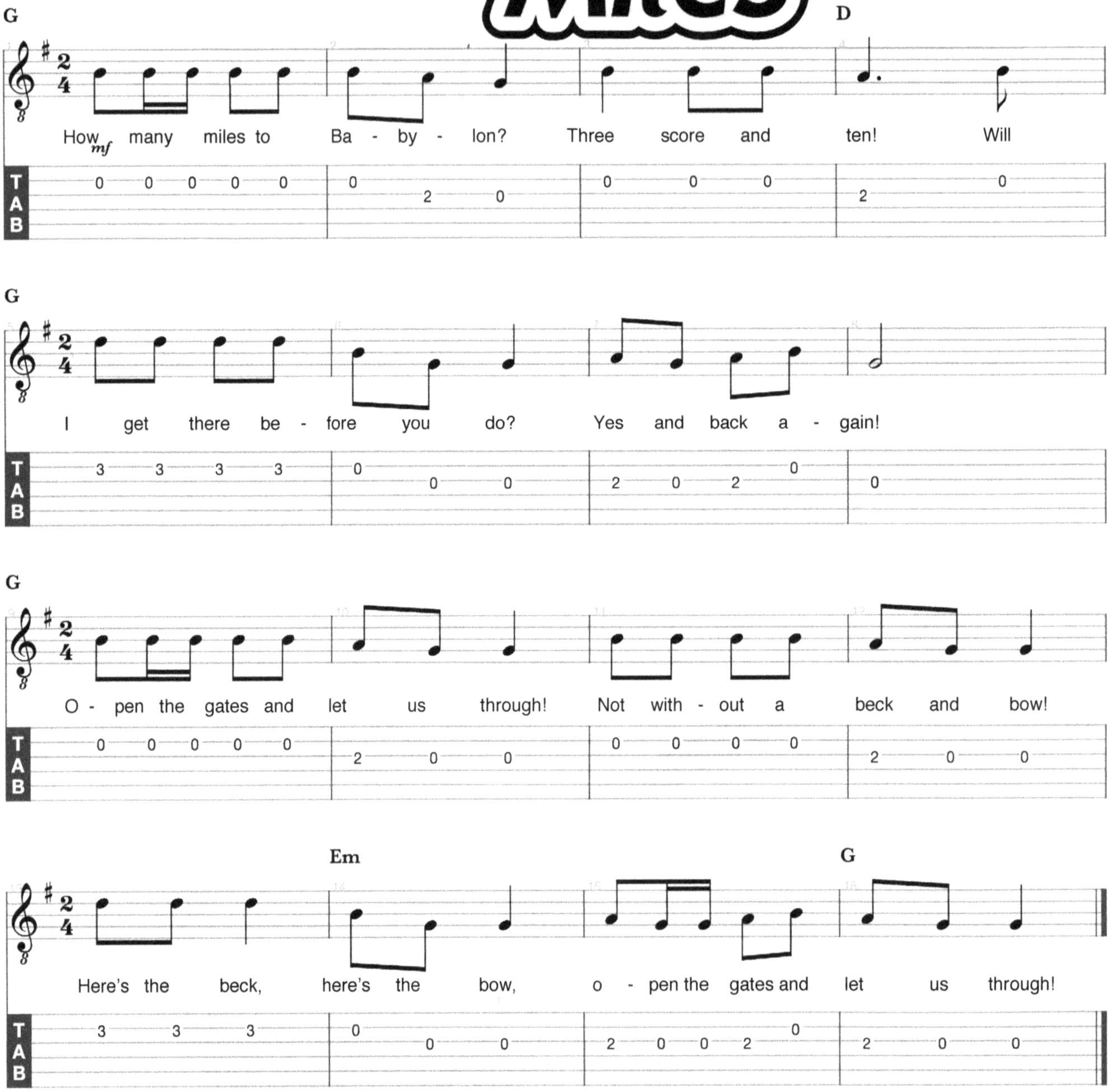

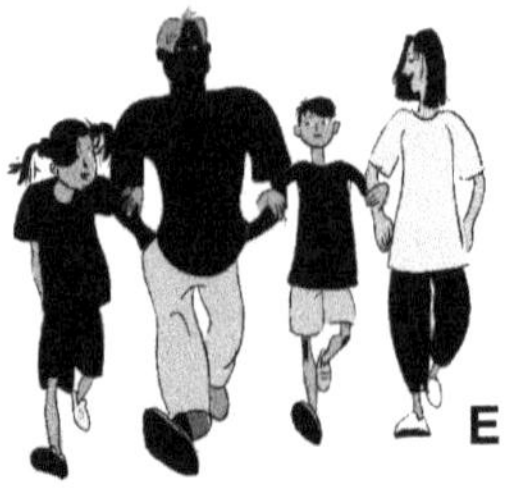

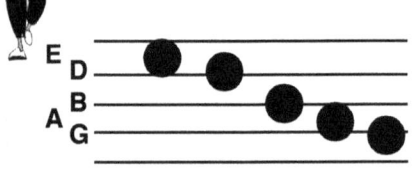

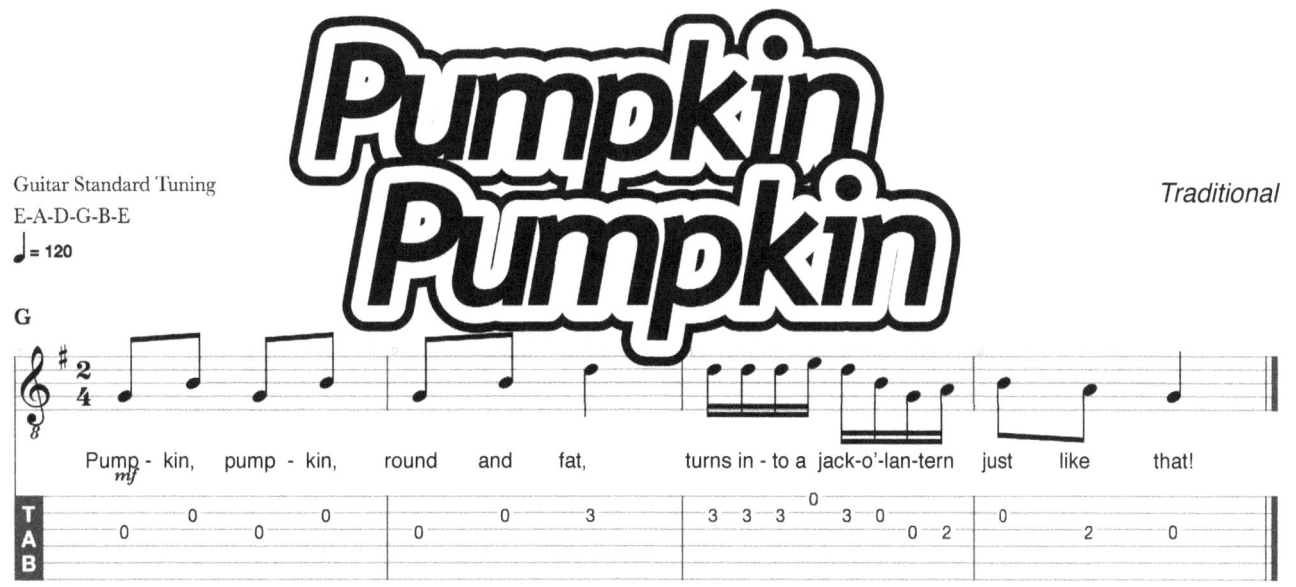

Guitar Standard Tuning
E-A-D-G-B-E
♩ = 120

Traditional

G

Pump - kin, pump - kin, round and fat, turns in - to a jack-o'-lan-tern just like that!

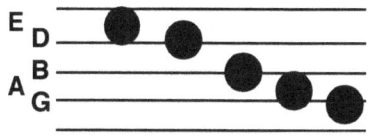

25

Built my Lady

Guitar Standard Tuning
E-A-D-G-B-E
♩= 120

Traditional

G

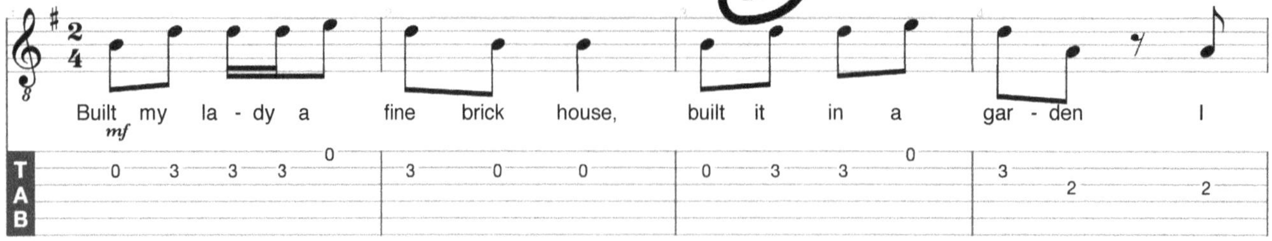

Built my la - dy a fine brick house, built it in a gar - den I
mf
T
A
B
0 3 3 3 0 3 0 0 0 3 3 0 3 2 2

G

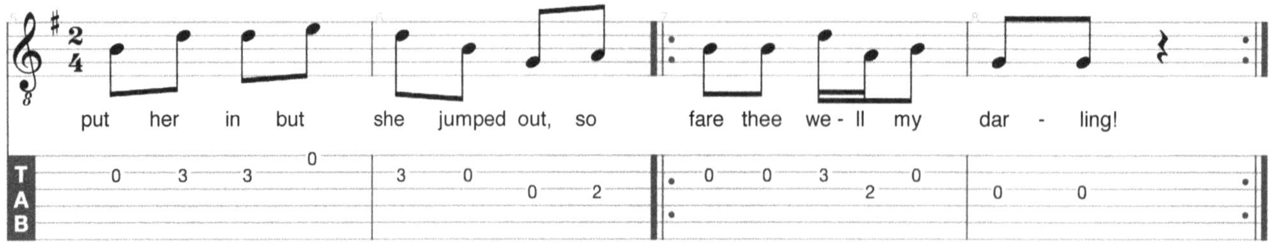

put her in but she jumped out, so fare thee we - ll my dar - ling!
T
A
B
0 3 3 0 3 0 0 2 0 0 3 2 0 0 0

Watch Out!

E
D
B
A
G

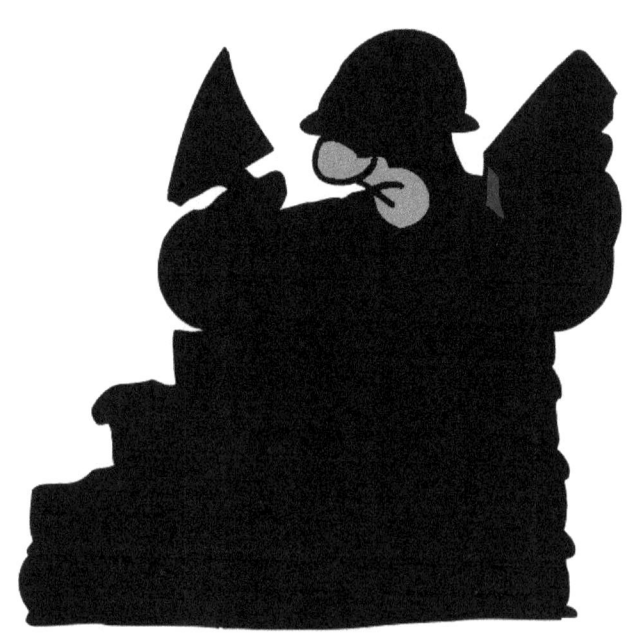

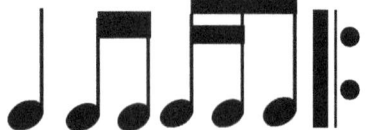

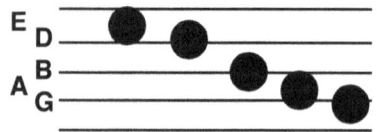

Guitar Standard Tuning
E-A-D-G-B-E
♩ = 120

Traditional

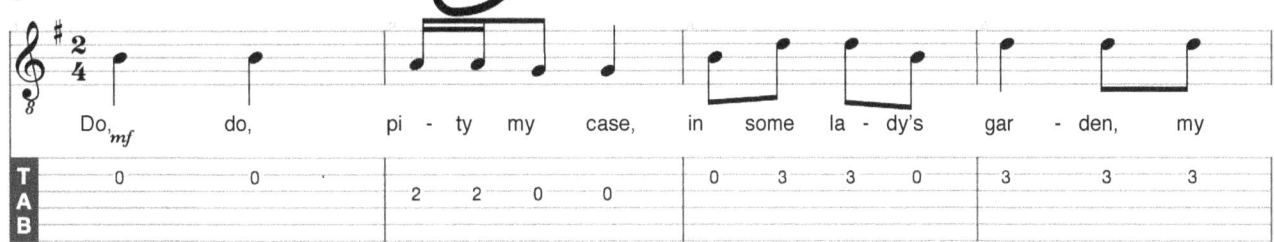

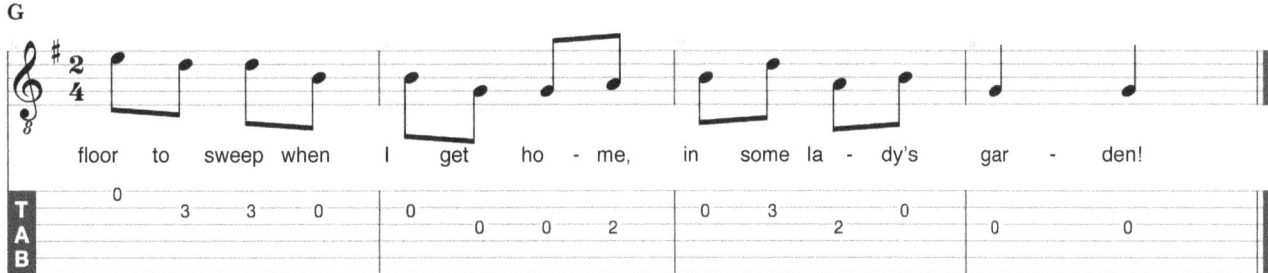

  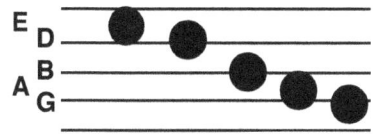

Down the Road

Guitar Standard Tuning
E-A-D-G-B-E
♩ = 120

Traditional

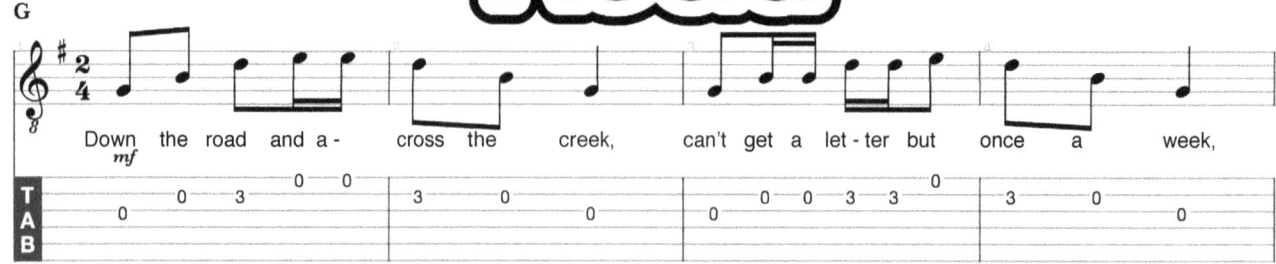

Down the road and a-cross the creek, can't get a let-ter but once a week,

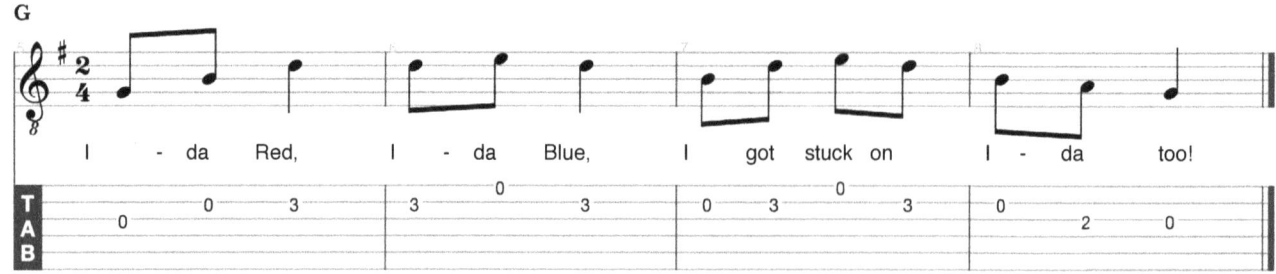

I-da Red, I-da Blue, I got stuck on I-da too!

Next verses:

Down the road and across the creek
Can't get a letter but once a week
Ida Red, Ida Yellow
She has got another fellow

Down the road and across the creek
Can't get a letter but once a week
Ida Red, Ida Green
Prettiest girl I've ever seen

Down the road and across the creek
Can't get a letter but once a week
Ida Red, Ida Brown
Prettiest girl that rode into town

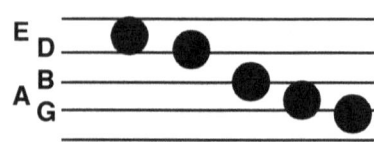

Guitar Standard Tuning
E-A-D-G-B-E
♩ = 120

Traditional

This Way Valerie

G

This way, Va - le - rie, that way, Va - le - rie, this way, Va - le - rie all day long!

mf

```
0           0           0
    3   3       3   3       3   3
0           0           0           0   2   0
```

G

Here comes a - no - ther one, just like the o - ther one, here come a - no - ther one, all, day long!

```
  0 0       0   0 0       0   0 0       0
      3 3         3 3         3 3
0           0           0           0   2   0
```

Watch Out!

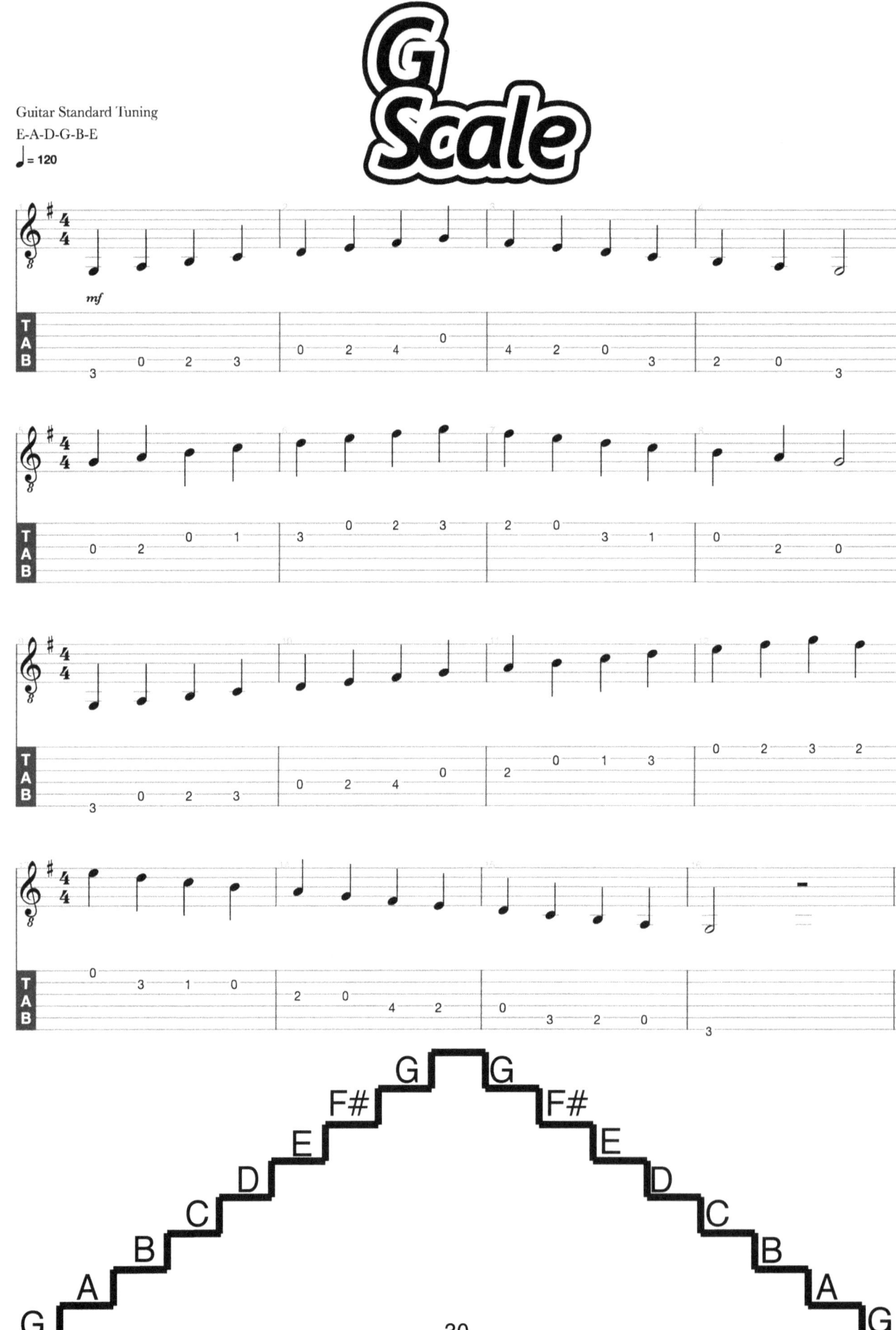

ABOUT THE AUTHOR

Frances has presented early years music sessions in a variety of settings since 2006, after training as a secondary mathematics and science teacher. She is fascinated by research into the health, educational and developmental benefits of music. Not content with being involved with children's music alone, she directs a local community choir, the Warblers.

AVAILABLE TITLES:

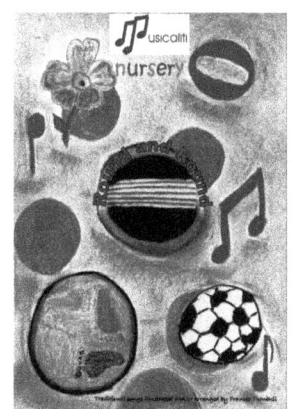

Musicaliti Nursery: Round and Round is a full-colour, illustrated book of well known children's songs for children. Each song includes music rhythms to which children can clap, tap, walk and sing.
ISBN: 978-1-907-935-008

Musicaliti Nursery Series: Magical Musical Kingdom is a full-colour, teaching series of well known and original children's songs with a royal element. Sessions include suggested instruments and activities, with an optional CD of music to purchase or download.
ISBN: 978-1-907-935-152

Musicaliti Nursery Series: Sharks, Fish, Shells is a full-colour, teaching series of well known and original children's songs with a fishy element. Sessions include suggested instruments and activities, with an optional CD of music to purchase or download.
ISBN: 978-1-907-935-169

Musicaliti Nursery Series: Yum, Yum, Yum! is a full-colour, teaching series of well known and original children's songs with a foody element. Sessions include suggested instruments and activities, with an optional CD of music to purchase or download.
ISBN: 978-1-907-935-206

Musicaliti Music Gone Wild is a full-colour, teaching series of well known and original children's songs with an animal element. Using ukulele instruction and chords, play along with your favourite animal songs today!

ISBN: 978-1-907-935-688

Musicaliti Goodies for Guitar is a full-colour, teaching series of well known and original children's songs for beginner guitar. With 90 songs both familiar and unfamiliar, this book covers songs in the scale of G, providing music notation, tablature and guitar chords for accompaniment.
ISBN: 978-1-907-935-206

FORTHCOMING TITLES:

Musicaliti Nursery Series: Balloons, Candles, Cake is a full-colour, teaching series of well known and original children's songs with a party element. Sessions include suggested instruments and activities, with an optional CD of music to purchase or download.
ISBN: 978-1-907-935-190

Musicaliti Nursery Series: Car, bike, plane is a full-colour, teaching series of well known and original children's songs with a transport element. Sessions include suggested instruments and activities, with an optional CD of music to purchase or download.

ISBN: 978-1-907-935-213

Follow Musicaliti NOW on FaceBook, LinkedIn, ReverbNation, SoundCloud, Twitter and YouTube!

www.ingramcontent.com/pod-product-compliance
Lightning Source LLC
Chambersburg PA
CBHW081940170426

43202CB00018B/2965